BIOGRAPHIES

# THURGOOD MARSHALL

by Lakita Wilson

PEBBLE
a capstone imprint

Pebble Explore is published by Pebble, an imprint of Capstone.
1710 Roe Crest Drive, North Mankato, Minnesota 56003
www.capstonepub.com

**Library of Congress Cataloging-in-Publication data is available
on the Library of Congress website.**
ISBN: 978-1-9771-1364-1 (library binding)
ISBN: 978-1-9771-1808-0 (paperback)
ISBN: 978-1-9771-1372-6 (eBook PDF)

Summary: Explores the life, challenges, and accomplishments of
U.S. Supreme Court Justice Thurgood Marshall.

**Image Credits**
Getty Images: Bachrach, cover, 1; iStockphoto: Kelvin Sterling Scott, 11;
LBJ Library: Yoichi Okamoto, 23, 29; Library of Congress: 7, 13, 17, 18, 21,
25; Newscom: Everett Collection, 27, World History Archive, 5, Zuma Press/
Keystone Pictures USA, 6; Shutterstock: Alex Landa (geometric background),
cover, back cover, 2, 29, Onur Ersin, 9, W. Scott McGill, 26; The New York
Public Library: 8; Wikimedia: FrancisNancy, 15

**Editorial Credits**
Erika L. Shores, editor; Elyse White, designer; Svetlana Zhurkin, media
researcher; Katy LaVigne, production specialist

All internet sites appearing in back matter were available and accurate when
this book was sent to press.

Printed and bound in China.
2489

# Table of Contents

Words in **bold** are in the glossary.

# Who Was Thurgood Marshall?

Thurgood Marshall was on the most important **court** in the United States. This is the U.S. **Supreme Court**. Before that, Thurgood won many **cases** as a **lawyer**. These cases changed the country's rules that had been unfair to African Americans. Thurgood said all Americans should have **equal** treatment.

# Childhood

Thurgood was born July 2, 1908. His mom was a teacher. His dad was a waiter on trains. Thurgood had an older brother named William. The family lived in Baltimore, Maryland.

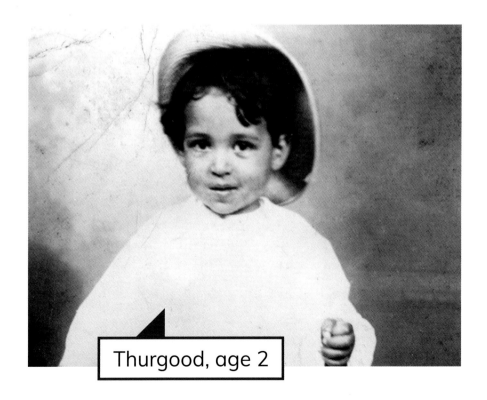

Thurgood, age 2

The city of Baltimore, Maryland, sometime between 1910 and 1920

Growing up, Thurgood saw black people treated badly. He knew black people were put in jail more and treated worse than white people. He knew black people had trouble finding jobs. Black people were also paid less than white people.

Thurgood's dad wanted his sons to know how the **law** worked. On his days off of work, he took them to the courthouse. They saw lawyers try to win cases. Back at home, Thurgood and his father talked about the cases.

Courthouse in Baltimore, Maryland

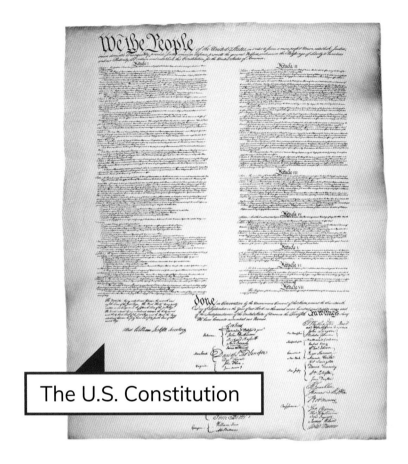

The U.S. Constitution

At times, Thurgood got in trouble at school. His teachers wanted him to be a better student. They made him learn the United States **Constitution**. It lists the **rights** of the people and the rules for the government. Thurgood knew every word by the time he left high school.

Thurgood went to Lincoln University in Pennsylvania. In 1930, Thurgood tried to go to law school in Maryland. The school did not let him in because he was black. Thurgood knew this was unfair. He instead went to Howard University Law School. It was a school for black people in Washington, D.C.

The library at
Howard University

In law school, Thurgood joined
a group that worked for **civil rights**.
It was called the National Association
for the Advancement of Colored People
(NAACP).

# Life's Work

Thurgood became a lawyer for the NAACP. In 1940, he worked on the *Smith v. Allwright* case. A black dentist named Dr. Lonnie Smith wanted to vote in Texas. But only white people in Texas had this right. To change this unfair law, Dr. Smith, Thurgood, and the NAACP needed to win their court case.

Thurgood took the case all the way to the Supreme Court. The court decided voting should be open to black people in Texas. This was a huge win. It was a step toward equal voting rights in the United States.

Thurgood around the time of the *Smith v. Allwright* case

In 1948, Thurgood became a lawyer on the *Shelley v. Kraemer* case. In this case, a white family sold their home to the Shelleys, a black family. White people who lived near the house were angry. They did not want to live near black people.

Thurgood again took the case to the Supreme Court. He said making the Shelleys move was against the law. The Supreme Court agreed. The Shelley family was able to live in the house.

The Shelley house is now a landmark in St. Louis, Missouri.

Black people in the United States were fed up with **separate but equal** laws. These laws kept black people and white people apart in schools, buses, and other places. But these things were not equal. White people got nicer things than black people.

Thurgood took a case called *Brown v. Board of Education* to the Supreme Court in 1954. He said *equal* meant getting the same thing, at the same time, in the same place. Equality could not happen if black and white children had their own schools. The court said the unfair law had to end.

Thurgood (middle) after the Supreme Court decided separate schools for black and white children were against the law

Thurgood (right) with other civil rights leaders in 1956

Some people didn't like Thurgood. They did not agree with his work for civil rights. One night he was picked up by the police for no reason. They drove Thurgood down a dark road. They knew a group of men was waiting there to kill him.

But two other lawyers and a news reporter had spotted Thurgood. They followed the police car. The group waiting to kill him didn't want to be seen breaking the law. They let Thurgood go.

Thurgood had more sadness in his life. His wife, Vivian "Buster" Burey, died in 1955 from cancer.

Thurgood then married Cecilia Suyat. Thurgood and Cecilia had two sons, Thurgood Jr. and John. They lived in Bethesda, Maryland.

Thurgood and Cecilia with their sons in 1961

# Supreme Court Justice

Thurgood had worked on 32 civil rights cases. He won 29 of them. These cases helped end unfair laws that kept black and white people apart. In 1967, President Lyndon B. Johnson chose Thurgood for the Supreme Court.

Some people didn't want Thurgood on the Supreme Court because he was black. But many people said Thurgood was smart and fair. On August 30, 1967, Thurgood became the first black U.S. Supreme Court justice.

On the Supreme Court, Thurgood decided cases that gave people equal rights. He helped protect the free speech of workers and students. These groups were afraid of losing their jobs or being kicked out of school if they spoke up. But Thurgood said the Constitution gives people the right to say what they think and not get in trouble for it.

Thurgood (far right) and the other
U.S. Supreme Court justices in 1976

Thurgood spent his life working for fairness. He helped change laws. He helped protect people under the Constitution.

The Thurgood Marshall monument in Annapolis, Maryland

Thurgood and Jomo Kenyatta,
the leader of Kenya, in Africa

Thurgood used what he learned from
the Constitution to help leaders in Africa.
These leaders were writing laws for
their countries. When Thurgood died
in 1993, his work had reached people
all over the world.

# Important Dates

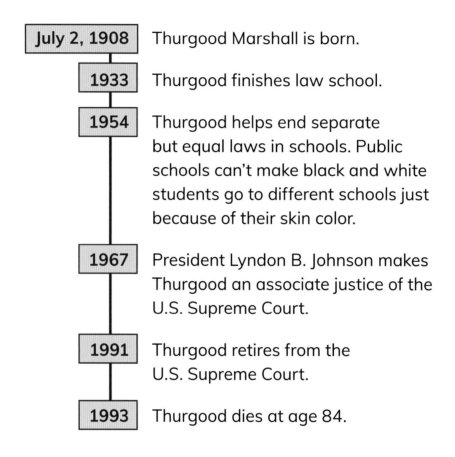

| | |
|---|---|
| **July 2, 1908** | Thurgood Marshall is born. |
| **1933** | Thurgood finishes law school. |
| **1954** | Thurgood helps end separate but equal laws in schools. Public schools can't make black and white students go to different schools just because of their skin color. |
| **1967** | President Lyndon B. Johnson makes Thurgood an associate justice of the U.S. Supreme Court. |
| **1991** | Thurgood retires from the U.S. Supreme Court. |
| **1993** | Thurgood dies at age 84. |

# Fast Facts

**Name:**
Thurgood Marshall

**Role:**
civil rights lawyer and
U.S. Supreme Court justice

**Life dates:**
July 2, 1908 to January 24, 1993

**Key accomplishments:**
Thurgood was the first black U.S. Supreme
Court justice. Before that he helped win
court cases for black American civil rights.

# Glossary

**case** (KAYS)—a question that is to be decided in court

**civil rights** (SI-vil RYTS)—the rights that all people have to freedom and equal treatment under the law

**Constitution** (kahn-stuh-TOO-shuhn)—the written system of laws in the United States that tells the rights of the people and the powers of the government

**court** (KORT)—a formal meeting in which facts are presented to a judge and often a jury so that decisions can be made according to the law

**equal** (EE-kwul)—being the same

**law** (LAW)—a set of rules made by the government that must be followed

**lawyer** (LAW-yur)—a person who helps people with law problems and speaks for them in court

**right** (RITE)—something that everyone should be able to do or to have and that the government shouldn't be able to take away, such as the right to speak freely

**separate but equal** (SEP-uh-rate BUT EE-kwuhl)—keeping people apart based on skin color but not giving the same things to all groups of people

**Supreme Court** (suh-PREEM KORT)—the most powerful court in the United States

# Read More

Sonneborn, Liz. *The Supreme Court: Why It Matters to You*. New York: Children's Press, 2019.

Stoltman, Joan. *Thurgood Marshall*. New York: Gareth Stevens Publishing, 2019.

Winter, Jonah, and Bryan Collier. *Thurgood*. New York: Schwartz & Wade Books, 2019.

# Internet Sites

*Thurgood Marshall*
http://www.historyforkids.net/thurgood-marshall.html

*Videos of Thurgood Marshall*
http://thurgoodmarshall.com/thurgood-marshall-videos/

# Index